Cats are sexy because they invented the meow.

MICHAEL P.

S E X Y   C A T

SEXY CATS

BY J.C. SUARÈS

TEXT BY JANA MARTIN

HarperResource

An Imprint of HarperCollinsPublishers

Copyright © 2000 by J.C. Suarès
Text copyright © 2000 by Jana Martin
Additional copyright information p. 80
All rights reserved, including the right of reproduction in whole or in part in any form.
CREATIVE DIRECTOR: J.C. Suarès
EDITOR AND PHOTO RESEARCHER: Jana Martin
DESIGNER: Hasmig M. Kacherian
All rights reserved. Printed in the United States of America. No part of this book may be used or reproduced in any manner whatsoever without written permission except in the case of brief quotations embodied in critical articles and reviews. For information address HarperCollins Publishers Inc., 10 East 53rd Street, New York, NY 10022.
HarperCollins books may be purchased for educational, business, or sales promotional use. For information please write: Special Markets Department, HarperCollins Publishers Inc., 10 East 53rd Street, New York, NY 10022.
FIRST EDITION
Library of Congress Cataloging-in-Publication Data
Suarès, Jean-Claude.
        Sexy cats/ by Jean-Claude Suarès.
        p. cm.
ISBN 0-688-17650-X
 1. Cats—Pictorial works. 2. Photography of cats. 3. Cats—Anecdotes. I. Title.
SF446 .S82 2000
636.8'0022'2—dc21
                                                                99-087610
00 01 02 03 04 QB 10 9 8 7 6 5 4 3 2 1
Thanks to the photographers and agencies for their images and stories, the animal trainers for their wisdom and anecdotes, the many cat owners for their tales and, finally, the Best Friends Animal Sanctuary in Kanab, Utah.

To Clint, Spooky, and Pigeon Willy, three sexy cats

HALF-TITLE PAGE:

CLAUDIA GORMAN

Curry Looking, Pleasant Valley, New York, 1996

FRONTISPIECE:

DENNIS MOSNER

Abyssinian, New York City, 1999

TITLE PAGE:

CLAUDIA GORMAN

Jake, New York City, 1997

FACING PAGE:

STUDIO PHOTOGRAPHER

Carole Lombard with Black Persian, Hollywood, 1931

INTRODUCTION

The sexiest cat I've ever seen on paper was in an advertisement. It was a black cat used to model jewelry sold by a now-defunct New York department store. He posed with his back to the camera, a slew of diamonds and pearls wrapped around his tail. I can't imagine any person in the world could look as sexy as he did: absolutely elegant, perfectly formed, self-possessed, mysterious.

In fact, cats have the whole act down pat. Between the look, the walk, the lounging around, and the primping, cats have been practicing how to be sexy for years.

The look: tiny mouth, tiny nose, big eyes, sleek coat, flat belly. If you took a pen to

JIM DRATFIELD/PAUL COUGHLIN
Alice in Pearls, Brooklyn, New York, 1995
"This Albino Siamese mix was hissing at me until I let her wear the pearls. Then she calmed down and started purring."

INTRODUCTION

paper and tried to design the sexiest animal on the planet, you'd end up with a cat.

Consider the colors they come in. Nature has bestowed more colors to the domestic house cat than to any other species. Black, orange, white, gray, fawn, chocolate, tortoiseshell, sable, to name a few. And some come in incredible, dazzling combinations: white cats with green eyes, orange cats with blue eyes. Have you ever seen a calico with eyes of two different colors?

The walk: cats can walk as gracefully as a runway model, full of restraint and confidence. They hardly ever lose their balance. They jump to high places with no apparent effort, rarely knocking anything over. If you watch your cat for years, perhaps someday you might become privy to the secret language of his tail. I have it on good authority that every movement means something, from enthusiasm to friendship.

INTRODUCTION

Lounging around: cats are the sexiest
accessories. They simply know how to pose
in such a way as to improve the look of
any chair, sofa, or bed. They'll never let you
catch them off guard: even half-asleep (which is
the most asleep they ever are), they manage to
look graceful no matter what. I have to confess I
once had a fat cat that snored,
but it was nothing like a dog's snore,
let alone my uncle Henry's.

The primping: cats know that to be sexy,
you have to be clean and smell good.
For that, they are willing to sacrifice a good
part of their day. Even the tiniest kittens know
to lick their coats clean and to wash
themselves behind the ears by wetting their
paws first. Can you think of another animal
who works so hard at being sexy?

— J.C. Suarès

Sexy is someone who'd rather lounge in bed all day than do anything else. Who knows how to give a little bite, moves like a dancer, and talks like a tramp. Who may have come from the alley but lives in a penthouse now. And lives on caviar, darling. So meet my cat.

ROBERTA MARCONI, RECORDING ARTIST MANAGER

PRECEDING PAGES:
JIM DRATFIELD/KEN CLARE
Russian Blue Reclining, Connecticut, 1996

CLAUDIA GORMAN
Curry in the Closet, Pleasant Valley, New York, 1997
"This is my cat, Curry, in the linen closet,
where he likes to spend his private moments."

A shadow bluer than a shadow, she came to him along the sill of the open glass window. There she stopped, staring at him, and did not jump down on Alain's chest until he continued to plead with her in words she knew well.

"Come, my little puma...my cat of high places, my lover of lilies. Saha, Saha, Saha...."

She resisted, seated above him on the windowsill. He could make out nothing about her but her cat outline against the sky, her dropped chin, her ears passionately turned in his direction; he was never able to catch unawares the expression in her eyes.

COLETTE

La Chatte

WALTER HODGES
Chumley in Hiding, Seattle, Washington, 1998

I got Cleo in Africa. She'd come into my life hungry and alone. She was so beautiful, it was love at first sight. I smuggled her back. Don't ask me how. For two days she stayed hidden in the bottom of my bag. Just slept. If she needed to go to the bathroom or eat, she never complained. She didn't do anything, really, for all that time. And I thought, to want to be with someone (or so I like to think) so badly, that you're willing to virtually stop living for a spell in order to get there? That's just amazing.

L. SAWAMBE, TEACHER

PRECEDING PAGES:

KRITINA LEE KNIEF
Alfie as Seducer, Broome Street, New York City, 1991
"She always knows full well the look she's giving you."

CLAUDIA GORMAN
Cassie, Pleasant Valley, New York, 1996
"Cassie, Curry's mother, in one of her seductive moods."

My Abyssinian taught me how to walk.

B. MARKLING, MODEL AND PERFORMANCE ARTIST

JIM DRATFIELD/KEN CLARE
Spencer as Wildcat, Connecticut, 1998
"We think he's a Ruddy Abyssinian, but he thinks he's a tiger."

Isabelle Francais
White Javanese, New York City, c.1997

Jayne Hinds Bidaut
Eroica Trio (Fudgie, Wudgie, and Rex), New York City, 1997

For if he meets another cat he will kiss her in kindness.

CHRISTOPHER SMART
"JUBILATE AGNO"

WAYNE EASTEP
The Apricot Brothers, Sarasota, Florida, c. 1996
"These flamepoint Siamese brothers were affectionate with all
of us. But they seemed to share a secret all their own."

ISABELLE FRANCAIS
Striped Egyptian Mau, New York City, 1998

ISABELLE FRANCAIS
Orange-striped Oriental, New York City, 1996
"These cats are the essence of exotic, except that they're absolute puppydogs when it comes to affection."

LAURENCE VETU-GALUD

Polish Girl and Chartreuse Cat, Neuilles, France, 1993

LAURENCE VETU-GALUD

Mimi, My Cat, with Model at the Fireplace, Paris, 1993

"Mimi wasn't supposed to be there. But he always gets in the picture.
He waits on the model's chair while she's getting her makeup on."

GEN NISHINO
Fidelity, Brooklyn, New York, 1994

ELLIOTT ERWITT
Fashion Plate, New York City, 1990

ABBAS
Prayer, the St. Paul Copt Monastery, Desert of the Red Sea, n.d.

STUDIO PHOTOGRAPHER
Christina Ricci and Her Costar in *That Darn Cat*, Hollywood, 1997
A Maine Coon was used for the remake of the 1965 original,
which starred Hayley Mills and a weighty Siamese named DC.

To please himself only the cat purrs.

PRECEDING PAGES:

HARRY GRUYAERT
Watching Out the Window, Amsterdam, Holland, 1999

DENNIS STOCK
Guitarist and White Cat, 1972

Five things I hear when I go Rollerblading with my cat on my shoulders:

1. Your cat's so handsome. What's his name?
2. We were just wondering where you got your cat.
3. Love your cat.
4. Does your cat like riding up there?
5. Who me? Oh, actually I wasn't looking at you, I was looking at your cat.

BRAD GURALNICK, SOUS-CHEF

PETER TIMMERMANS
Tabby Turns to Gold, Vancouver, Canada, 1996
"This is my daughter's cat. He sat down in a ray of sun in our backyard and turned into a king."

KARL BADEN

Misha, Boston, Massachusetts, 1999

"Misha belongs to some friends of ours. He's a small and tidy guy who hardly ever leaves the house, particularly since he looks bigger sitting in the window."

Ah! cats are a mysterious kind of folk.
There is more passing in their minds than
we are aware of. It comes no doubt from
their being too familiar with warlocks and
witches.

SIR WALTER SCOTT

LAURENCE VETU-GALUD
Mimi the Illegal Alien, New York City, 1995
"He always takes a strategic position, so he can look out the
window and cover my work at the same time."

At the age of six I developed a mad, crazy crush on Sophia Loren. I'd seen her on television in some movie. My father thought it was cute. So he said, "You know what makes her so beautiful? Look at her eyes. She's part cat."

I believed him for years. Even now I'm half convinced.

CHUCK WALSH, CYCLING COACH

SIMON CHERPITEL
Tuxedoed Cat with Yellow Eyes, 1972

GILLES PERESS

Cat on a Railing, 1998

PAULETTE BRAUN

Gorgeous Max, Sarasota, Florida, 1994

He's a tomcattin' man,
Can't stop his sinnin' round.
He's a tomcattin' man,
Can't stop his sinnin' round.
The women all callin'
Come into my house.

ANONYMOUS
BLUES LYRIC, 1920s

SEXY

50

CATS

WAYNE MILLER
Young Tabby, 1964

He delighted to roam about the garden, and stroll among the trees, and to lie on the green grass and luxuriate in all the sweet influences of summer. You could never accuse him of idleness, and yet he knew the secret of repose.

CHARLES DUDLEY WARNER
"CALVIN"

MICHAEL NICHOLS
Sleep, 1995

MARIA PAPE
Green-Eyed Cat, 1992

JEAN PRAGEN
Tortoiseshell, Sweden, 1989

I find Eloise is always in a better mood after a vigorous stroking, a rich meal—perhaps of oysters or lobster—and a sip or two of champagne. Then perhaps a walk in the garden where she can nibble on a few pansies and chase a bumblebee with absolutely no intention of really catching it. And then dessert: crème brulée? A nip of fine chocolate? Strawberry sorbet? You never know—she likes variety. The vet might frown on it, but we all have to relax somehow.   **S. GOMERSBY, ORIENTAL RUG IMPORTER**

KRITINA LEE KNIEF
Sasha in the Garden of Love, Pennsylvania, 1993
"He's the feline equivalent of Adam; a cat so majestic you might think all other cats are merely his descendants."

PRECEDING PAGES:

INGE MORATH
On the Venetian Steps, Venice, Italy, 1956

WHITE HOUSE PHOTOGRAPHER
Socks on the White House Lawn, Washington, DC, 1993

LEONARD FREED
Temporary Still Life, Garrison, New York, 1995

My cats—Elvis and God—are already seductive beings by virtue of their names alone. But I've always called them sexy. They're curious and naughty, and they like to lie voluptuously around.

E. McDONNELL, JOURNALIST

KRITINA LEE KNIEF
Spongie, Upstate New York, 1990
"He was an absolute cuddlebug, so spongy and squeezable that you immediately knew how he got his name."

I got a cat so I'd have more appeal to women.

B. SHANKLE, CARPENTER

PRECEDING PAGES:

CLAUDIA GORMAN
Want Me, Love Me, Feed Me, Pleasant Valley, 1997

PHILIPPE HALSMAN
Gina Lollobrigida with Persian, New York City, 1954

STUDIO PHOTOGRAPHER
Ann-Margret and Siamese Kitten, Hollywood, 1964

POPPERFOTO
Jean Harlow and Cream Persian, Hollywood, 1930s

STUDIO PHOTOGRAPHER
Kim Novak and Pyewacket the Siamese, Costars in *Bell, Book and Candle*, Hollywood, 1958

STUDIO PHOTOGRAPHER
Audrey Hepburn as Holly Golightly and Orangey as "Cat,"
Costars in *Breakfast at Tiffany's*, Hollywood, 1961

And hand in hand, on the edge of the
sand,
  They danced by the light of the moon,
  The moon,
  The moon,
They danced by the light of the moon.

EDWARD LEAR
"THE OWL AND THE PUSSYCAT"

HELENE TORESDOTTER
My Friend Petra Holding Gaston, Malmö, Sweden, 1987

DENNIS MOSNER
Domestic Shorthair, New York City, 1999
"She responded best to singing. She completely ignored my treats."

LINDA RASKIN
Sheba, New York City, 1979
"I was supposed to be photographing a model in the lobby, but Sheba, watching from the staircase, caught my eye. When the film came back from the lab, the model was forgotten. The cat was the winner."

ERIC LARRAYADIEU
What Is Night, c. 1990

There is, indeed, no single quality of the cat that man could not emulate to his advantage.

CARL VAN VECHTEN
THE TIGER IN THE HOUSE

HARRY MUNRO
Frankie the Office Manager, Kanab, Utah, 1998
"At the Best Friends Animal Sanctuary, a friendly place, Frankie maintains a certain elegant distance, which makes guests all the more interested in knowing him."

Photo Credits

© Abbas/Magnum Photos, p. 34
© Archive Photos, pp. 68, 69
© Karl Baden, pp. 42–43
© Jayne Hinds Bidaut, p. 25
© Paulette Braun, p. 49
© Simon Cherpitel/Magnum Photos, p. 47
© Tony David, p. 6
© Disney Enterprises, Inc., courtesy The Kobal Collection, p. 35
© Jim Dratfield's Petography, Inc., front cover, pp. 8, 12–13, 23
© Nina Duran, p. 6
© Wayne Eastep/Tony Stone Images, p. 27
© Elliott Erwitt/Magnum Photos, p. 33
© Isabelle Francais, pp. 24, 28, 29
© Leonard Freed/Magnum Photos, p. 61
© Claudia Gorman, pp. 2–3, title page, 15, 21, 64–65
© Harry Gruyaert/Magnum Photos, p. 36–37
Philippe Halsman © Yvonne Halsman, p. 67
© Walter Hodges/Tony Stone Images, p. 17
© Kritina Lee Knief, pp. 18–19, 57, 63
Courtesy The Kobal Collection, pp. 7, 70, 71
© Eric Larrayadieu/Tony Stone Images, p. 77
© Wayne Miller/Magnum Photos, p. 51
© Inge Morath/Magnum Photos, pp. 58–59
© Dennis Mosner, pp. 1, 75
© Harry Munro for Best Friends Animal Sanctuary, Kanab, Utah, p. 79
© Michael Nichols/Magnum Photos, p. 53
© Gen Nishino/Tony Stone Images, p. 32
© Maria Pape/FPG Int'l LLC, p. 54
© Gilles Peress/Magnum Photos, p. 48
© Jean Pragen/Tony Stone Images, p. 55
© Linda Raskin/Liaison Agency p. 76
© Dennis Stock/Magnum Photos, p. 39
© Peter Timmermans/Tony Stone Images, p. 41
© Helene Toresdotter/Tiofoto, p. 73
© Laurence Vetu-Galud, pp. 30, 31, 45
Courtesy The White House, p. 60
Excerpt on page 16 from Colette, *La Chatte* (The Cat), translated by Morris Bentnick.
Copyright © 1936 Farrar & Rinehart, Inc.

SEXY

80

CATS